Our *Divine* Magnificence

SHARI SHEA

BALBOA.PRESS
A DIVISION OF HAY HOUSE

Balboa Press books may be ordered through
booksellers or by contacting:

Balboa Press
A Division of Hay House
1663 Liberty Drive
Bloomington, IN 47403
www.balboapress.com
844-682-1282

Because of the dynamic nature of the Internet, any web
addresses or links contained in this book may have changed
since publication and may no longer be valid. The views
expressed in this work are solely those of the author and do
not necessarily reflect the views of the publisher, and the
publisher hereby disclaims any responsibility for them.

The author of this book does not dispense medical advice or
prescribe the use of any technique as a form of treatment for
physical, emotional, or medical problems without the advice
of a physician, either directly or indirectly. The intent of the
author is only to offer information of a general nature to help
you in your quest for emotional and spiritual well-being.
In the event you use any of the information in this book for
yourself, which is your constitutional right, the author and
the publisher assume no responsibility for your actions.

Any people depicted in stock imagery provided by
Getty Images are models, and such images are
being used for illustrative purposes only.
Certain stock imagery © Getty Images.

Print information available on the last page.

ISBN: 978-1-9822-5976-1 (sc)
ISBN: 978-1-9822-5977-8 (e)

Balboa Press rev. date: 12/10/2020

Dedication

To my Beloved Holy Spirit Creator of all, with my deepest heartfelt gratitude for EVERYTHING! You walk with me through each and every life experience and Illuminate my being with ever expansive Love and Grace. I have given my life to you in Holy Sacred Service, and am forever Blessed to know and live the intimate depth of our Divine Union, in this life and beyond...

Contents

Acknowledgements

With great love and appreciation for my life partner and husband, Bob. When the stars aligned, so too began our family, with years of adventures and memories that have enriched our life experiences. We have supported one another with growth in our own unique ways, while also holding dear our united source of connection.

My children Ryan and Holly plus daughter-in-law Teresa who have continued "saving mom" from tech overload. Their support with all of my computer work, including social media, has and is profoundly appreciated. Thank you for being "lights" in my life. I love you dearly.

Mom and Dad continue to encourage me with love, words of wisdom and sound advice; even if sometimes I need to take the road less traveled. Much love I feel for you both.

My sisters Carin and San. So many joyful memories we have made through the years. We have shared difficult experiences over the years and have been there to support one another and always will. I love you my sisters.

With Deep Gratitude for Padre Paul, who has been and continues to be a devoted mentor and teacher for me. Padre's love for God is evident in his daily walk. He has modeled for me deeper "surrender," be still and listen to hear the voice of Holy Spirit. Within this listening process, a clarity comes through which lights the path of direction. He calls this, the "mind of God" merging with our indwelling presence.

Bishop Dana speaks with Elder Wisdom which helps me find redirection when I slip and falter. He works in Devotional Service with Guidance and Love for all who seek truth. I truly appreciate my Spiritual Brother.

Bishop Bobee evokes healing with joy and has helped me became aware of insights not clear to me. He emanates compassionate service for those who seek it. I truly appreciate my Spiritual Brother.

Reverend Carolyn for our Kindred Spirit connection, and her welcoming me into service with her congregation.

Anne for her gracious skills with typing and editing this book.

My daughter Holly, who shot the front and back cover of this book with her skilled photography.

Foreword

We all have this sense that the place we are living spiritually is too small to accommodate the bigger picture God has planted inside each of us. There has to be more, there has to be a process we can follow, or a mentor to look up to, to point the way for our hearts to follow. Like the "Star of David" in the Christmas story, God leads three Wisemen to the very birthplace of the promised Messiah foretold hundreds of years before through the prophets.

This same yearning of following the Light of God continues to draw us to life experiences that change the course or directions in following the will of God. These seekings or travelings have taken us to places we would never dream about until that still small voice within leads us to a place of transformation.

In *Our Divine Magnificence*, you will find stories of Shari's travels that take her spirit on many adventures as she seeks her Spiritual Truth and finds a deeper understanding of this LIGHT that is within her. Shari's adventures lead her to people of spiritual influence that created this Divine Spark that lives in her now. They also helped her become courageous in stepping out with her own spiritual gifts after learning the power of Decrees and Faith that shaped her life and ministry in the years that followed.

I have watched and observed Shari's growth over the years and her unquenchable desire to manifest this "Divine Presence" for healing in her own life and Ministry is remarkable. Shari motivates the reader with time tested quotes that spark our own curiosity to venture into the unknown and seek our heart's desire that the Creator has planted deep within our souls.

Padre Paul Funfsinn
Spiritual Shephard of Celebrating Life Ministries
www.CelebratingLifeMinistries.com

Introduction

We are here for a Holy Purpose. We are at the Aligned Place, at the Aligned Time, in this Present Moment. I have written this book with the encouragement and Guidance of my Beloved Creator and amazing Spiritual Team of Master Teachers along with Saints, Archangel Raphael and my Guardian Angel – STAR. The following teachings, stories and Spiritual Growth lessons are for all seekers of Truth, Passion and Purpose.

It is crucial given the times that are now upon us to grow more deeply in relationship with the Source of our being. Our Spiritual Teams are a wonderful Blessing and can help us with Divine connection. We must however, not let them become a replacement for our Beloved Creator. They must not become False Gods or Gurus, if we are to continue moving forward with Cosmic Truth. At some point we must bravely make direct contact with our Inner Sanctuary.

I use many names in this book referring to "the Allness of Everything" or God, which many of you can relate to. Some of these words are Beloved, Creator, Holy Spirit, Divine Presence, Source. These names personally feel more expansive for me when expressing my thoughts. You will see me use them interchangeably throughout this book. You the reader will use what is most comfortable for you.

When Jesus said, "He that is without sin among you, let him first cast a stone" this is because he knew that this lesson would speak to us throughout all time. Let us remember, as our world is greatly changing before our eyes to see this unfolding process through the eyes of Love, non-judgement and non-attachment. The high awareness to seek is that Creator is everything.

For some of you the words within these pages may be reminders of previous learnings that are instilled within your being, which you may feel in your heart to be truth. For others these words may evoke an awakening for which a new journey of learning may unfold. For each one of us our journeys and interpretations may vary, but our destination remains the same. Deep within our being we yearn to know our Beloved in an intimate spiritual relationship and our Beloved yearns for this as well. It is through this bond of Grace that we are made Whole.

Chapter 1

Reclaim your Spiritual Power

I was guided to begin my book with this most profound and powerful statement by the late Ron Roth; one of my greatest spiritual teachers and co-founder of Celebrating Life Ministries.

> *We all have locked deep within us a spiritual power that holds the key to our healing. We have only to follow a few simple steps that are essential to liberating the spiritual energy that may lie dormant within us.*

This statement by Ron, makes me want to shout out to the rooftops "It is within us! Wake up oh ye sleeper!"

What is Spiritual Power? I believe it is the power to Manifest all that we Desire. This includes our Divine Birthright, to live and be whole/well – Emotionally, Spiritually and Physically.

We need to find a form of prayer, meditation, or contemplation and take a few minutes to be still each day. As we pause and go within to meet the presence of our being, our purpose and destiny can be revealed to us. We can then rejoice in sharing our talents, gifts, and graces in service to ourselves and humanity; as well as create a loving relationship with Divine Intelligence.

As we continue moving towards Reclaiming Our Spiritual Power, we are wise to be aware of the following: Our thoughts Create our Beliefs and Attitudes. Our Beliefs and Attitudes create our circumstances and outcomes in our lives. So, what are we thinking? What thoughts have we instilled in our consciousness as Beliefs and Attitudes? I shared in my first book, *Living in Grace*, a powerful experience and physical health imbalance, that became my healing journey. You see, I had created disharmony in my body through "negative thoughts held with feeling."

As I adapted new patterns of "positive" thoughts held with feeling, including meditation and increased nutrition, my physical, emotional and spiritual bodies were brought back to balance and harmony. I was no longer in need of the surgery that was prescribed for me. Doctors would call this a "Miracle." I call it spontaneous Spiritual Healing. Through my process of dis-ease (lack of ease) I lived as though I were well. I focused on the "I am" principles that we can apply to any and every situation/circumstance or challenge in our life. My mantra during those few weeks of healing were: "I am well." "I am perfect health." "I am whole."

All around us is an expansive vortex of energy. We have the ability to open our consciousness to higher states of vibration. In these higher vibratory states, we can access the cosmos, and unleash Spiritual Power for our highest potential. We must always remember to decree with feeling and conviction what we desire and relinquish any strong hold we may have on how, when, and where these desires will manifest.

We have the power within our being of choosing to "lovingly release" all thoughts, beliefs, and behaviors that are no longer supporting us in our life. It does not matter how long we have held onto them; we can begin now by an act of the will to let them go. This may require a paradigm shift. The source of our being is helping us to move from upside down to right side up. It takes dedication and practice to BE the Victorious Being that you are intended to be!

When I was just 17 years old, a devastating tornado ripped through my neighborhood in Windsor, Connecticut. The tornado was too close to the radar to be detected at our nearby Bradley International Airport weather station. We, therefore, had no warning before its touchdown.

Just minutes before the tornado was upon my neighborhood, my mother had gone upstairs to our kitchen to get me some ice cream. Seconds after she handed it to me, the winds began to howl as though a freight train was barreling through our house. The noise was so loud that I jumped up from the couch where I had been sitting. My mother and I huddled in our downstairs hallway hugging one another, as windows broke around us. This freight train sounding noise was so unbearably loud. Rain began to pour outside with such intensity, that we could not see out of the windows. As my mom and I embraced one another in sheer terror, we uttered the words "this might be the end of the world."

In an attempt to reach out for help, mom picked up the receiver from the wall phone next to us. She dialed zero for the operator and told the woman on the other end what was happening. My mother's words to the operator were, "I think we may be having a tornado here in Windsor." It was just moments before this call that I got a glimpse through a window downstairs. I could see at that point that our neighbor's home across the street, was no longer standing. This is how my mother had concluded and voiced a tornado possibility to the operator on the phone. The operator's response was a sarcastic "Oh really?" My mother's next thought was to call my father at his office. She had a brief conversation with him, of only a minute or two, explaining what was happening. Dad told us to hang tight and he would head home.

What had seemed like an hour of fright and terror, had in fact, only been a few minutes. The unbearably loud noise had ended, but the rains continued with monsoon intensity. The reality of what had occurred was just beginning to set in. My mother, in sadness, revealed that her friend Carol, our neighbor across the street, had stayed home sick from work that day. Seeing her house leveled to the ground (and my mother fearing that Carol may have been resting upstairs in her bedroom), brought a great sadness upon us.

In the days, weeks, and months ahead we, along with many other families in our neighborhood, lived in trailers that were placed in our front yards. This was due to many of us losing part or all of our homes from this devastating tornado. The ceilings and walls of our living and dining rooms, along with our kitchen ceiling had all blown away with the tornado. Our neighbor Carol, had in fact, been blown out of her home and was killed. She was found in the backyard home of our neighbor's two houses down. We were in great sorrow for Carol and her family's loss.

The terror I felt from this experience caused me to have nightmares on and off for a number of years. Rain and thunderstorms, which I had once felt excitement for, I now dreaded and became afraid when they occurred. This went on for about a decade. I can remember bringing my small children down to our basement, with snacks, toys and a port-a-potty, whenever the winds began to pick up for a thunderstorm. We would stay down there until the storm passed.

It was not until I was in my early forties that I made the conscious choice to address my fear. At that time, I began to develop a deeper trust in a higher power. A loving presence that worked with me through faith and grace. It was through developing a relationship with this Presence that I was led to see my fear could be released. I no longer needed to be controlled by these feelings, but that the power was within me to FREE myself from this bondage. Through meditation, contemplation and prayer I reclaimed my Spiritual Power. From that point on I began to love the thrill and excitement of rain, wind, and thunderstorms once again.

Chapter 2

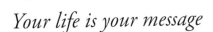

Your life is your message

One of Mahatma Gandhi's well know quotes is "My life is my message." This has come to be my favorite of his quotes, and one that I aspire to in my daily walk.

While there is a lot of responsibility that comes with this aspiration, it is both a joy and commitment to be mindful of one's behaviors in life. In the words of Ron Roth, it is "Spiritual Maturity" to live one's message. If we are willing to view our behaviors in this way, then the following will help us assess how we are progressing. To live our message, we must be in Love and Balance. While we all falter at times due to the human nature part of our being, through meditation, prayer and devotion we can rise to find restoration and harmony. With this in mind I give you three ideas to ponder.

A first idea to ponder is: How do we treat ourselves? What does our self-talk sound like? Do we take care of our physical body with adequate nutrition, exercise and sleep? Do we have time for relaxation, enjoyment, meditation, and prayer? Are we pursuing, in some fashion, something that we are Passionate about, a calling, heart-felt desire? If so, have we begun, or are we already sharing this with humanity? While these are many questions to ponder, they are all important for our overall wellbeing.

A second idea to ponder is: How do we treat others; our brothers and sisters of humanity? Are we regularly harsh, judgmental, opinionated, too talkative, abusive, dismissive, etc.? While some of these words may sound harsh, many of us can relate to at least a few of them. If we are in fact expressing any of these on a regular basis, we can work to release their energy and rise to loving complimentary, and empowering replacements.

A third idea to ponder is: How do we act and react in situations that may feel out of sync, or be upsetting to us? Do we react with anger, rage, jealousy, foul language, stomping, pouting, etc.? If our answer is yes to any of these, the ten second rule before responding, works well. I have used it myself on many occasions. It helps one take pause, stop, feel and listen to the inner thoughts, feelings and emotions welling up inside. It is during these ten seconds that we are empowered with CHOICE. The choice to BLAST or FAST.

While we know what I mean by BLAST, the alternative FAST, opens a new door, allowing one to feel the emotions without the need to vent them at the present time. This gives time to rethink/reevaluate later. More than not for me, having this pause to settle down and regroup puts things in a new and different perspective. It also enables me to later have a rational conversation and share how I was impacted.

Along with these three ideas mentioned, I have found the following to be staples in my life for many years now.

- Hang out with people that are happy more than they are unhappy.
- Listen to positive uplifting music that speaks to your soul, whatever that may be for you.

- Chose television programs and movies wisely.

We all have a different threshold of what inspires, us, and what may throw our vibration off. It is important that you listen carefully to the inner guidance and wisdom that will reveal this balance.

While you may not have expected this chapter "Your Life is Your Message," to flow in this way, it felt important for me to share with you how I have been able to look and "see" the ways in which I am living my message and how these changes helped me. When we remain open and act on the guidance we receive from within our being, our "message" and way of living and being is heard, seen, and felt by others in tangible ways. We become a Beacon of Light, and a model for others of what is possible for all of us. When we live what we preach, we are living a Spirit Directed Life. A statement in the book, *The 12 Powers* says, "I am a radiating center of Love." We are all love and can live this way. When Gandhi said, "Be the Change You Wish to See in the World," I feel he meant Arise oh ye sleeper and take up your place in the hearts of women and men. Don't die with your boots on!

I shall end this chapter with a piece written by Bessie Stanley, an American writer from the late 1800's, which was mistakenly attributed to Ralph Waldo Emerson because he was more well known. This is my favorite piece of writing that I refer to often.

> *To laugh often and much. To win the respect of intelligent people and the affection of children. To earn the appreciation of honest critics and endure the betrayal of false friends; to appreciate beauty, to find the best in others; to leave the world a bit better, whether by a healthy child, a garden patch, or a redeemed social condition; to know even one life has breathed easier because you have lived. This is to have succeeded.*

Chapter 3

Follow your Heart

I believe there is a Sacred Space and place in each one of us, that is near the physical heart. While I am not referring to our physically beating heart, this Sacred Chamber is nearby. We have all heard the saying "Follow your Heart." While some believe it is nonsense to not rely on one's brain for decision making; others have a deep abiding trust, often without even knowing why, to listen to what the heart may reveal. While yet others are more passionate with tapping into their solar plexus (area in the gut) for answers.

My higher guidance has shared with me that the Sacred Chamber, which I made mention of above, holds within it the grand intelligence of everything. Our brain does not hold a candle to the wisdom and expansiveness of this Holy Ground. Each one of us who experience this space, whether in daily life or through meditation and prayer, KNOW the vastness of ALL that is held there.

We can meet with Divine Presence in this Holy Chamber. It is here that we merge as one in the present moment, as time and space dissolve. The most profound relationship of our life with Presence can grow and evolve here. This strength within can support us through every joy, sorrow, and seeming obstacle that may come upon us. Your life has Holy Purpose.

When we look to the light within, we will receive the guidance that we seek with balance. This includes the rationale guidance for self-preservation, such as looking both ways before crossing the street. The clarity when making choices for our life and matters is revealed with truth, even if it may not be what we want to hear.

The brain is ego based, and the physical heart is feeling based. The sacred intelligence within however, is unbiased and nonjudgmental. It seeks to reveal only truth that is aligned for our highest evolutionary process at the present time. As truth and guidance are revealed to us, it may be through thoughts, hunches, and ideas. We may feel led to read a certain book, call or email a specific person. There may be a word, phrase or sentence on a television program, movie, in a magazine, or on a billboard sign that speaks to us personally. We may have an ah-ha moment, as this is what we have been waiting for. We need to pay attention to these inner thoughts, hunches, and ideas, as they are avenues to help us move forward with a knowing that all is well.

Remember, we all have our own individual and unique places where we tap in and BE with the Sacredness of our being. For some of us it's outdoors, in nature, for some a private prayer closet or sanctuary, for others who have been tuning in for many years, it can be anywhere, anytime. It may not matter where or the volume of noise around them, for they have mastered living continually with this Presence.

I will leave you with this piece spoken by Gary Zukov form his book titled *The Seat of the Soul*, abbreviated.

> *The soul is what we are. It is a powerful, purposeful essence. It is at the very center of who we are.*

Our soul is enormous. It existed before we were born and will exist after we die. For the soul never dies. It is like our mothership that knows all. Our job is to learn how to sail our little boat and choose to go in the same direction as our mothership. When we do sail in the same direction life fills with meaning and purpose, with love and excitement to be alive, excited about people you are with, and what you are doing. "Meaning" is our inner compass that always aligns itself with direction, of where the mother ship wants us to go.

Chapter 4

Reach for the Stars

Theodore Roosevelt, our 26th President said: Believe you can and you're halfway there." To me "believing that we can" have, acquire, be gifted with all that we desire, is referring to "Having Faith" even as small as a mustard seed. I ask now, how far are you and I willing to reach for our stars? What is our comfort level? Of course, it's different for all of us, but how much are you willing to risk, to live and to be your authentic self, no matter what your age?

Ask yourself how have others, including yourself, over the years discouraged you from reaching too far? Have you been afraid of what others may think, or how you may be perceived for striving outside of the box? If so, I strongly encourage you now to let all of that go if you want to experience true happiness and bliss in your life.

There is an inner drive in each and every one of us to be and do great things. These great things are both what we would consider big and small. From lending someone a helping hand to leading Congress in a Nationwide effort to slow Global Warming. The little acts of kindness, such as a smile to someone seeming in need, are just as important as one may perceive the expressions of bigger acts to be. Mother Teresa used to say "we have so many people who want to do the 'big' things in this world. We need many more to do the 'little' things that matter just as much."

Brian Tracy says: "Move out of your comfort zone. You can only grow if you are willing to feel awkward and uncomfortable when you try something new." I ask you, is your cup half full or half empty? Helen Keller said, "Life is either a daring adventure or nothing. To keep our faces toward change and behave like free spirits in the presence of fate is strength undefeatable." What an awesome proclamation from a woman with so many physical limitations in her life. Her words here are a testament to how her "faith of a mustard seed" helped her learn and eventually thrive in a world that posed great challenges for her.

Challenges arrive in our life no matter who we are or where we are in our life. One such example occurred at 5:30 in the evening on December 10, 1914 when a massive explosion erupted in West Orange, New Jersey. Ten factory buildings in a plant that belonged to Thomas Edison were engulfed in flames. Edison's son Charles walked over to him as they watched flames eat away his life's work. In a childlike manner Thomas said to his 24-year-old son, "go and get your mother and all of her friends. They will never see a fire like this again." When Charles objected, Edison said, "It's all right. We've just gotten rid of a lot of rubbish." He later said, "although I am over 67 years old, I will start all over again tomorrow."

Wow, he was such a courageous man who reached for the stars, was an accomplished inventor, and even in his later years, never let age or the hardship of losing ten manufacturing plants stand in his way. We too can find this inner strength and the courage to pursue our dreams, no matter how big or small they may seem to us. When we are willing to risk it all for our passions and destiny a whole new world of promise will lead the way. At the core of our being it is the in-dweller who supports and guides our every move.

Since the title of this chapter is Reach for the Stars, I want to end it with something that was shared in a Hallmark movie from 2013, entitled *Finding Christmas.* In the movie, while on a hayride, a woman speaks these words to her beau:

> *90% of our body mass is stardust. All of the same elements except hydrogen and helium are found in the stars. We are all connected – everything is tied together. When you feel disconnected just look up. You are the Universe expressing itself. It is impossible to be separated. If you sit still, you can feel it all around you.*

Chapter 5

Raise your Vibration

We are living in a time of heightened Spiritual Awakening and Awareness, to our True Nature as Spirit Beings. Powerful Cosmic Light and Energy are entering our planet now. They carry a High Vibrational Vortex. We have the opportunity to tap into this Cosmic Light Consciousness, raise in vibration, and BE the Love that we are. In order to live in these higher states of consciousness we may need to evaluate and modify some of our behaviors and habits. As we begin to flow with this shifting process, we can consciously pay attention to how we are feeling in each moment. It is important to be honest when asking ourselves questions such as:

1. Are we focused on mostly eating foods that provide our bodies with energy and vitality?

2. Are we exercising our limbs, joints and muscles, for optimal balance and strength throughout our life? By eating vital foods and keeping our bodies in decent functionality we help our cells and organs rejuvenate, balance and stabilize for our overall wellbeing.

3. What are we feeding our minds and thoughts? It is equally important to strive for thoughts and feelings that promote joy, peace, and clear thinking. Our emotional wellbeing depends on it. Meditation, contemplation, and prayer are three processes that can help us live in emotional balance and flow.

I invite you now to take pause from reading this chapter for a few minutes. Listen to your body, mind and spirit. Intuitively evaluate yourself and make some notes of how you are feeling in these areas. You may need to make some changes, moderate some foods and behaviors for optimal balance. I do this practice regularly for myself and make changes and tweaks frequently. I am trying to be a constant listener to the needs of my being.

Dictionary.com online shares the following definition for the word vibration: motion, quiver, tremor. Emanation sensed by those who are attuned to it. Most of us have had physical and sense experiences with vibration. When someone walks into a room where we are, we can often, especially when we are paying attention, feel light or heavy energy. This may come to us as recognizing the individual without looking at them to know who is there; this feeling is coming from a person's vibration. We can become aware of vibrations we are holding at any given time AND through Spiritual Discipline, alter them. By this I mean change them if need be.

This feels to be the perfect time to share a piece written by Emerson, which speaks about our sole. He writes:

> *Within us is the soul of the whole.*
> *The wise silence to which every*
> *part and particle is equally related;*
> *the eternal one. When it breaks*
> *through our intellect it is Genius.*
> *When it breaks through our will, it*
> *is Virtue. When it flows through our*

> *affections it is love. To experience this place is a passion like no other. So intense is this passion that it can weave a dream into reality, bring Heaven to Earth, Liberate the Slave, heal the sick, and bring forth wonders never before dreamed.*

This piece can refresh our being and bring us back to this very present moment, the here and now.

There are Spiritual Laws of Vibration that I came across online. They are very easy to understand, and reminders for us, when we slip, miss the mark, or fall off track. Anger and rage are low vibrational energies. Fear is a heavy vibration, and often underlies them with a sense of powerlessness and vulnerability. Through choice, however, we can bring into our field of vibration, peace, calmness, love, harmony, light, etc. and our vibration will rise. When we believe negative self-talk, whether self-imposed or directed towards us by others, we can dip into a level whereby emanating heavy and dark vibrations. We can tap into our power within and BE our authentic self. When we choose to forgive ourselves and others through compassion, love and joy we can transmute these dark and heavy vibrations. A high self-worth and confidence emits high frequency light energies, which lift our vibrations considerably. We then act as Masters of the Light and radiate this light to others, uplifting our vibrations and the vibrations of those around us.

Lastly, thoughts held with feelings of jealousy, resentment and unforgiveness carry very heavy vibrations that can lead to Illness and Disease. They block our Life Force Energy. The wonderful news is, that healing can occur when high frequency energy is channeled to that person. This can happen in several ways.

1. Through one's own will and desire to be well.
2. Lifestyle changes.
3. Others praying for you, whether in person or distance healing.
4. Visualization of seeing one's body whole and enjoying activities one may no longer have been able to participate in.
5. Or a combination of all or some of the above.

There are so many other ways that channel high vibrational energy, through positive thinking and healing, which can transmute the heavy vibrational energy of illness. This transmutation allows the body to return to its natural state of wholeness. I call this Returning to Grace. This state of Grace is available for all of us.

Chapter 6

Face It, Feel It, Give It

Our son, Ryan, married our beautiful daughter-in-law, Teresa, two years ago. At that time, and now, we have been so grateful that they found one another and are deeply in love. I had an experience during their wedding that surprised me, and it offered an opportunity for deep healing.

While many parents shed some tears and reminisce at their child's wedding, what came up for me was one of the most painful episodes of my life. The ceremony was outside under a lovely veranda. Shortly after the Bride and Groom's families were seated, I looked over at Ryan as he waited for his Bride. We were only about twenty feet from one another. I found myself just staring at him. Thoughts of great joy overcame me, that he was to marry such a wonderful young woman who understood and accepted all of him. This is every parent's dream. Ryan turned and looked at me as I continued gazing at him. I smiled and blew him a kiss, and he blew one back to me. In that very instant I felt as though the earth was crumbling beneath me. My consciousness became engulfed with the most dreadful sorrow I have ever felt in my life. I just wanted to scream and yell at the top of my lungs. My eyes filled with puddles of tears which made me very thankful for the waterproof makeup that I was wearing. Instead of asking myself what was going on I listened to my guidance which echoed this mantra of Face It, Feel It, Give It. I did not pause to even question what that meant, I just trusted the process. I knew intuitively I was to face that my son has grown up. My son is standing here on his wedding day waiting for his Bride. He has another woman, who would be the most important one, to take care of him, and share everything with. I was no longer first in his life. I realized that he would no longer be waiting for the special Saturday chocolate chip pancake breakfast or a special mom made sandwich, I would create when he stopped by for lunch during the time he worked nearby. He is a lucky guy whose wife loves doing these things for the both of them. Special confidential chats that we had frequently shared, in our close bond, would now be shared with his Bride.

The sheer pain that I felt in my heart, as I Faced all of this, hit me as though Ryan had died and was no longer in a physical form. While I had had moments of tears, during Ryan and Teresa's one-year engagement, with the understanding that things would change, I did not realize just how ATTACHED I was to my son. I knew I had to Face It, Feel It and Give It.

With regards to <u>Face It</u>: We must be willing to see the things in our life, whether past or present, that are in our way and preventing us from living "CLEAR" in the flow of life. These "things" that I am referring to can be in our conscious or subconscious mind. In this situation for me, the attachment to my son was in my subconscious, buried down deep.

With regards to <u>Feel It:</u> We must be willing to feel these emotions, experiences, and heartaches. As we allow our feelings to come forth, we can hold and cradle them as one would a baby. Hold and rock them gently. I honored myself feeling their vibration and how I was triggered by these feelings. To feel my emotions, as painful as they were, at my son's wedding helped me with this healing process and I did the best I could under the circumstances. I did not want to share these feelings with everyone attending to the wedding as Teresa was about to walk down the aisle, so I was unable to give it my full attention. I believe this is why these difficult feelings came to the forefront two more times on their wedding day. Those additional times both occurred during Ryan and Teresa's wedding reception which followed the ceremony.

I was triggered by my emotions again during their first dance and special song "Perfect" by Ed Sheeran. Then shortly thereafter for the third time. The same feelings of sorrow, dread, loneliness, etc. came over me. My sister, San, was sitting next to me, and lent a comforting presence for me to Face It, Feel It, and finally be able to Give It!

With regards to Give It: This is the third and final piece of this healing process. This is the Glorious time to "GIVE" all the baggage and attachments that no longer serve us to the Source-Universal Energy. They no longer belong to us. As we release them, we do so with love...

as they have helped us grow and have shown us a New Way.

I love this statement from PersonalGrowth. com, as our personal responsibility for healing. It says: "What you do today is important, because you're exchanging a day of your life for it." I add to it this statement: "so choose wisely."

Chapter 7

My Mary Magdalene Pilgrimage

I had been attending classes and reading on the life and work of Mary Magdalene for several years. I was intrigued and inspired by her Faith, courage, and healing abilities. My studies began in 2010. By May of 2018, I would find myself on a most Holy and Sacred Pilgrimage to France following in her footsteps, and essence, while deeply learning about her work.

Before I share some of my Pilgrimage with you, I wish to explain some things about her, things that some people are still unaware of. I myself, having been raised in the Catholic Faith, grew up believing that Mary Magdalene was a Prostitute whom Jesus healed of demonic control. Let's begin here and clear up some misconceptions that have tainted her persona for a very long time.

The Bible, as many of us are aware, depicts Mary as a lowly prostitute. She has been spoken of in this manner by many Priests for countless years. It was not until centuries later, in 1969, that the Catholic Church retracted this idea, which rolled back centuries of labeling her as such.

In 2017, our present Pope, Pope Francis, declared a major Feast Day of July 22nd in honor of her life and work. He went on to say that Mary Magdalene was a true authentic Evangelizer and declared her as Apostle of the Apostles. He then stated that she showed love for Christ and she was much loved by Christ. He spoke of Jesus' love and grace toward Mary, who had been exploited and despised by men who thought they were righteous. Although I came upon this information a couple of years ago, I had known in my heart and studied other writings about her that corroborated this newer piece of writing.

From my readings and teachings, I learned that Mary was gifted with abilities as a young child. She connected very deeply with all of nature, both in day and night. It was in these times of communion that she received wisdom and grace, with following her path of Spiritual Growth and maturity. At some point before reaching adulthood, she received training in the Ancient Healing Practices. Some writings depict this training to have taken place in Egypt. After a few years of training she returned home to Bethany. It was at that time that she knew her destiny would be to work with and follow Jesus of Nazareth. We all have our own "inner knowing" and/or "beliefs" regarding the widespread writings about Jesus and Mary Magdalene being married and having children together. I am however, not going to dip in with my personal guidance ether way in this book. I wish only to be one more soul who is helping to make credible this Powerful devoted woman who served the light with unwavering Faith and asked for nothing in return.

After the ordeal in Jerusalem with the conviction of Jesus, etc. Mary Magdalene, some family and others fled and sailed to Southern France. Many writings and stories place Mary landing in Sainte-Maries-de-la-Mer, France. It was from this quaint fishing village that my pilgrimage began.

The internal guidance I was receiving in

2017, caused my pilgrimage to become reality in May of 2018. This pilgrimage was to be a private one with just one of my dear friends, Lorraine. After a car ride to JFK and a several hour flight we landed in Marseille, France. We picked up our rental SUV, and drove the two-hour ride to Sainte-Maries-de-la-Mer. While planning this journey it was made clear that we should visit and experience three different sites on our week-long stay. I heard 'begin at the beginning' and for me this meant where Mary first landed, Sainte-Maries-de-la-Mer, France. Our hotel was right across the street from the ocean in this quaint village. I asked our hotel attendant if there was knowledge on the appropriate area where it had been said the landing occurred. Everyone in this village is very knowledgeable about Mary's legend, and they all honor her for her work with humanity. She told me that the landing occurred between the hotels Camille, which is a charming modern-day hotel where we stayed, and hotel L'Abrivado. We walked on the boardwalk that day, but the evening hour was upon us, so I decided to wait until the next morning to spend time on the beach. I was overcome with excitement and anticipation, which made it difficult to fall asleep as night fell.

I eventually found sleep and the next morning, I awoke bright and early. Lorraine and I each had some food that we had packed for our trip which served as our morning meal. Once breakfast was behind me, without hesitation, I made the short walk to the beach. I received guidance from within, that Mary and the others landed closer to the hotel L'Abrivado, so I crossed the street and found a spot near the water. At that hour I was the only one there. I laid out a small towel on the sand and began meditating as the waves softly rolled up on the shore. I began to imagine the hardship Mary and the others must have endured, first from the ordeal in Jerusalem, and then the long journey to a foreign land. At the same time, I pictured in my mind's eye, the boats landing in the harbor, and I wanted so profoundly to feel her presence. Alas, I did not. I was, however, so very grateful for that first morning's Blessing in that Sacred Land.

As early afternoon began, Lorraine and I met up and experienced the towns' outdoor shops and restaurants. Just being in this area carried a Sacred Vibration that sustained a lightness within my being. It was as though an inner knowing without "Knowing" anything specific. I could not stop smiling and expressing fruitful joy!

The next morning, I awoke bright and early once again. I had a light breakfast and made my way back down to the beach. I laid my little towel down at about the same spot as the morning before. Before beginning my meditation, I felt guided to collect a few shells from the sea's edge, and wade into the surf a bit, up to ankle deep water. It gave chills to my body as the outside temperature was only around 65 degrees. As I made my way back to sit on the towel, I brought to mind some things I had read about this small fishing village with a population of 2,048 people which I will share below.

The ocean waters in Sainte Marie are said to be infused with several thousand years of prayers and healings. People have stepped in these waters for purification and ritual, bringing them in Divine Union with Creator/Source. The purification ritual is a form of cleansing and preparedness for the next step in one's Holy service in this life. After a time of reflection, I made the intention to tap into the essence of Mary Magdalene. This time around it did not take long and within a minute or so I began to feel her presence all about my being. I felt so loved and could feel how much she appreciated the long journey I had made to connect with her. As I sat and felt her Holy Essence with me, we communed, and I was shown a glimpse of her parties landing on that beach after their long journey from Israel. Tired and weary were they, but joyful for their new connections in Sainte Marie for certain people in this village had received word and were expecting them. This was to be a whole new beginning for Mary and those who joined her on this journey. A fresh new start and an expansion of her Healing Ministry were to begin in this land.

As I continued being with her essence for a while longer, profound feelings of joy and gratitude came over me. Tears began to gently fall about my face. I am not sure how much time I spent communing with Mary for the next thing I knew, my friend Lorraine was calling to me from the boardwalk. I ran to her as she met me on the beach. I put my arms out, hugged her tightly, and told her that Mary was with me. The timing of my experiences here were perfect as at that point we needed to check out of our hotel room.

From Sainte-Maries-de-la-Mer we headed to the town of Sainte Maximin. It is said that this is one of the areas where Mary performed many miraculous healings of the Spirit. We stayed at the Hotel Le Couvent Royal, a former monastery to Monks for hundreds of years. Our room was upstairs in a long hallway with many sleeping rooms on either side. The energy from the Monks who had lived there was palpable.

In this hotel, the downstairs door from a side lobby to the outdoor courtyard was literally fifty feet high and six inches thick. It brought laughter to our expressions as we opened it to the inner courtyard. Inside the courtyard is home to dozens of birds who flutter all about from tree to tree. They have nests all around in the eaves and fill the air with their joyful songs.

Walking about this quaint provincial little French Town, one can feel the flair and style of the French culture. All of the windows are shuttered and uniquely colored, as are the houses and businesses. There are no screens in the windows. I took a photo of a cat sitting on the outside ledge of an open shuttered window, at his home. It was so lovely to take in a new culture, so very different from my own in the United States, and to be in the energy of the area.

This feels like the perfect time to share with

you some of what I myself have learned about the work of Mary Magdalene. Mary and her team of healers traveled and worked in South and Southwest France. Mary had trained in the art of healing through the use of medicinal oils. I know many people today who incorporate these oils with their healing work. I am one of them. Frankincense and Pure Rose Oil are two such oils that carry a high vibration and can aide with healing. I always wear these oils on my body and hands before facilitating, and when attending, healing events. Padre Paul Funfsinn, head of a healing ministry I am part of, and his team, Dana and Bobee, use healing balms for rituals, such as Sacred Baptism and hands on healing, in a manner similar to what Mary Magdalene did. As Mary worked with Holy Spirit in these rituals and healings on behalf of others, trapped emotions of pain, sorrow, unforgiveness, etc. were released. Although we are in modern times today, these same types of healings take place with Padre Paul Funfsinn and his team during Healing Services with Celebrating Life Ministries.

The locals in St. Maximim/St. Baume France speak of Mary and her team working in a particular area of Southwest France called

Remes les Bains. They worked by healing river waters that are said to carry a high intelligence and vibration. The waters would take the trapped emotions of people that she was working with and purify them as they were washed away. We would have loved to have visited this area, but it would have been an additional five-hour drive.

Over the years I have placed crystals in a stream close to my Vermont home, and watched them wash downstream whereby purifying the waters with Sacred energy. Mary worked with what are known as "Essence Teachings" that were lived by the Therapeutae, who were known for their healing abilities in the ancient Greek world. Ron Roth, Co-founder of Celebrating Life Ministries with Paul Funfsinn, spoke often of the Therapeutae at retreats I attended. Ron said that the Therapeutae would walk from town to town, and as they did so, people would be healed just from being in their presence. Ron and Paul incorporated these Sacred Healing elements, just as Mary had done so. Although this chapter is about Mary, it is believed by many that Jesus was at the helm in working this way and he was a mentor for Mary. Mary taught "The Way," as she called it, of Love, Faith, and community that changed lives at the core of their being. She is a treasured gift whose strength, courage and wisdom lives on forever.

Our third and final site to visit was the cave at the Holy Mountain in Sainte Baume. This cave is said to be where Mary spent the last several years of her life praying and healing people. Again, the locals at these sites speak of her with reverence. There are many statues throughout South and Southwest France depicting Mary teaching and preaching.

We stayed at the hotel in Sainte Maximim during our two-day visits to the cave. The first day we had decided to visit the lovely church, referred to as a Basilica in this part of the world, next to our hotel. It is richly adorned with paintings, carvings and statues. Some of them are of Mary Magdalene. There is a crypt in the lower level that people can walk into where there is an encased skull that is said to be that of Mary Magdalene. The hotel, which is a former monastery, and the Basilica were both built in 1295 by Charles II, King of Sicily, Count of Provence. The Basilica was built to house the relics of Mary, as legend says that her body was discovered in an ancient crypt directly underneath it in 1279. I did not, however, feel that the skull on display was that of Mary.

I was so excited to experience the cave at Sainte Baume, and that afternoon we ventured to it. Dare I say that it was a twenty minute or so drive, but our GPS kept kicking out, which had the unintended consequence of taking us quite a bit longer than planned to arrive at the site. At some point along the way I relieved Lorraine of the driving. Little did either one of us know, that we would be driving up the cliff of a mountain to reach an area, where one could hike up much higher, to the cave. I believe that I did overcome some fear of heights after experiencing those narrow and curvy roads. At certain points where the trees made an opening, Lorraine said that she could see straight down.

Once we reached our destination and parked, we popped into the little gift shop, which was adorned with many Mary Magdalene treasures. At last, it was time for our hike up to the cave. There were a few different paths that one could choose from to hike up to our destination. Unbeknownst to us, we chose to take the most difficult path with lots of rocks and tree roots. What a blessing that was, for what lay before us was an "Enchanted Forest" of sorts. I began to feel that I had embodied Snow White from my favorite childhood fairytale. The trees were so tall and ancient looking. Their trunks were so large and mighty with massive roots all about the ground. Emerald green moss covered parts of their trunks and roots. One such trunk was shaped like a foot at the bottom. The stubs coming out from it looked like toes. This tree embodied a "Gentle Giant" welcoming us in. I felt so light and airy as a child in purest joy. A mushroom seemed to grab my attention as it sat perfectly in the center of a hollowed hole tree stump. In one area some rocks were naturally piled up on one another, with vines growing all about them. They formed what looked to be a forest bench. Holly bushes, wildflowers and herbs laid as bedding adorning the path sides. The birds were singing joyously with angelic harmony and tone rejoicing in our arrival. It was as though the gateway to another dimension had opened for us to pass through, and the welcoming party was illuminating! As the "Enchanted Forest" came to an end, we then had a little further uphill trek on a paved path, which led us to the cave. I felt such peace in my heart and immense gratitude to finally be upon this third, and in my mind, most treasured site.

Mary's Grotto is inside the cave. It is said that her Grotto is still potent with her presence, and it is surrounded by countless Angels. As I made my way into the cave I began to tremble while feeling I had entered a Holy Temple surrounded by Mary's presence. I decided to make my way down to the lower level, where Mary's Grotto was, as it was getting to be later in the day, with visitors needing to leave by dusk. As I entered this space, I went over to a bench in front of a stone statue that is made in Mary's image. I could feel powerful energy and vibration all around me. I became a little weepy to finally have reached the destination that had been calling me for so long.

I glanced around at one corner of the Grotto where water was dripping from the ceiling. We visited the Grotto during the mud season which meant that we were one of the few pilgrims in attendance; most wait for summer months to avoid the mud season. After a few minutes of contemplation, I decided to take some photos of her grotto and the upper level of the cave. We would be returning the next day, which was a Sunday, and I planned to sit longer with Mary's essence then.

On the upper level of the cave, there is an Altar where services are frequently held, and several chairs are about. There are a few statues of Mary around on that level, candles available for purchase, and a glass box encased with bones, said to be that of Mary. There is an area in the upper level where water drips down pretty heavily from the cave. The water is said to be Holy and Blessed. People can fill their water bottles if they wish to. Before too long we made our way back down the mountain path with a few other pilgrims visiting the site.

The next morning, I awoke bright and early. We got ourselves fed, backpacks set and drove back to Sainte Baume Mountain. We chose a different path to walk up this time. Although it did not have the same energy as the "Enchanted Forest" one, it was easy to hike and much faster. I was feeling great anticipation on this day, as I knew we would have all the time we desired to be in Mary's presence.

We had finally arrived at the cave door once again and I felt compelled to go straight down to Mary's Grotto. Lorraine stayed outside the cave for a little while, enjoying the view and lavish sunshine. I was the only person down in Mary's Grotto for several minutes and was drawn to, once again, find the bench placed near her statue. Three votive candles had been placed at this statue and their light set a powerful healing tone in the atmosphere that surrounded me. As I gazed lovingly at this statue I said to Mary's essence "I have come so far to see you." Tears filled my eyes then, as they do now as I share this experience with you. While I sat in this space, surrendered, humbled, and honored, I began to sob like a child. I cried and cried and cried for at least 15 minutes. I felt so loved, and present in that space. The essence of Mary was showering me with healing Grace and attuning me with great Blessings for the next level of my healing work. She had called me to her Grotto just when I was ready to receive these most sacred gifts.

When my tears finally subsided and I came to myself, I realized that at some point Lorraine had come down to sit with me. I took this time to walk over to the dripping water in the cave's corner, filling the three small plastic waterproof containers that I had packed at home for collecting Holy Water. I also gathered some of the pebble stones in the basin to use in Healing Services. As I sat back down on the Grotto bench, a Sacred Mass began in the upper level. The Priest was reciting the mass in French, which held a magical vibration for me as if I were understanding a language that I had never spoken before. When people began singing, we felt the Grace of Heaven upon us. We stayed in the Grotto and experienced about half of the service. At that point the journey was complete, and I am forever Changed and Graced.

Chapter 8

Be the Love That You Are

We have come from <u>Love</u>. We live as <u>Love</u> and one day we shall return to <u>Love.</u> This is the truth of our being. It is our choice however, to live and be this Love that we Are!

Each of us have a Sacred Contract with the Source of our being. Part of this contract is our agreement with Creator, to express and serve humanity with specific gifts and graces, that our Spirit is ready to share. Sometimes we deny our gifts by refusing, for various reasons, to serve others. Other times, we may not be consciously aware of what our gifts are. Many people spend years trying to "figure out" their souls' purpose in life. It is in the "human egoic" trying, that we fail. Unity Minister, Reverend Phil Smedstad used to say, "Surrender Sooner."

The most painless way to seek guidance or signs of direction from the Source of our being is through the act of taking a little time to pray, meditate or contemplate. Using one's ego to find these answers can lead to one becoming "full of one's self" leaving one to feel better, more Blessed/Gifted than another. It can make us the opposite of humble and if we are not careful, we can crumble. "Ego" in the sense of conceit is a low vibration and unauthentic. At some point egoic based ideas fall apart.

The category that I fell into several years ago was being closed off to hearing the Holy Spirit speaking to me. This often times happens when one is very happy living their life in a certain way; they may be closed off to the "more" that is awaiting them to do/be. In my case, as it is for others, a health challenge/imbalance may be needed as a "wake up call." For me it was physical but also had spiritual and emotional elements as well. I talk about this time in my life in my first book, so to suffice in this one, I will just reiterate that in the end, and my new beginning, this experience was one of the greatest Blessings of my life. It shook me at the core and guided me to go within, whereby forming a relationship with Creator that showed me that I was called to healing work.

I share with you now, this beautiful piece written by Michael Tamura, a celebrated spiritual leader, from his book entitled *You are the answer.*

It is from love that we are born and to love we must return. This is the journey of the soul that we call life. To be who we are, to have all that is within us, and to fully express our Divine Heritage. That is our purpose and destination of our journey. Spiritual Growth is the process of fulfilling this purpose - and is nowhere to be found, but here within us now. For our Destiny is Freedom. As we learn to choose truth at every crossroads, and act upon it with love – we begin to enter into the Sacred Divine with life – and experience the joy of our own existence.

And I add that the key for all is the "entering in." We can do and be nothing without co-creating a relationship with the Source of our being. It begins with an intention, our will, and yearning. As we become silent, we enter into this quiet place and ask for guidance, listen and allow this Sacred time to grow. Like the seeds we plant and water for fruit, so too this Divine relationship needs to be tended to every day. It is our Spiritual Responsibility.

In Glenda Green's book *Love without End: Jesus Speaks,* there are some quotes that Glenda states were shared with her by Jesus in meetings they had together. Here are a few of them.

Jesus Speaks:

> *Love has no opposites.*
> *Kindness is the heart of living. It is what makes life bearable, meaningful and delicious.*
> *There are no structures that cannot be superseded and rearranged by love.*
> *Love is your true self, which springs forth from God, the indefinable everlasting fountain of existence.*
> *Everything was created in innocence. Behold this if you would see the face of God.*
> *The highest unity is one which respects differences as well as sameness and regards both with equal respect.*

*When you are being the love that
you are you realize that the secret
of success already exists in the
nature of your beingness.*

*God's will abides in truth. Know
the truth, and you will know the
will of God. The heart knows truth
as that which sets it free.*

The Universe is implicitly and explicitly of one piece.

Being in the heart is prayer.

As a man loves, so he is. As he believes, so he becomes.

We can affirm with conviction and mindfulness together here and now to be and live the love that we are.

HALLELULIA, PRESENCE LIVES IN US ALL!

Chapter 9

The Expansion of Celebrating Life Ministries (CLM)

As I shared briefly in my first book, *Living in Grace*, Paul Funfsinn, whom we affectionally and reverently call "Padre" has been leading and mentoring people with this ministry for several years. I have been part of this Sacred Order since attending my first retreat in April of 2004.

Padre has many gifts of the spirit, including clairvoyance, clairaudience and clairsentient which come through him and guide people in profound ways, during Healing Services and event retreats that CLM facilitates. It is through Holy Spirit that he reads hearts as well as people's life experiences. He sees energy blocks that can prevent one from healing. These blocks can be emotional, spiritual, physical or any single/combination of them.

Padre's heart is filled with love for God and his fellow man. Padre sees Christ in everyone as Jesus expressed in his life and continues to do so in essence. When Padre teaches and speaks, he is fully tapped into the Holy and Sacred Divine Presence. As the words of wisdom come through Padre's being with sheer elegant simplicity and humility, my heart melts as I am touched by the hand of Grace.

Padre encourages all of us to go deeper in relationship with the Source of our being and work towards being and living with this Presence throughout our days and nights. Padre says that when we achieve this for ourselves a whole new world will await us. He goes on to say that we will have taken the burdens, cares, and concerns of our life and hand them to God. From here we must then get out of the way, referring to our egoic minds, and allow Holy Spirit to guide us. We will never have to feel that we are "alone" in the world again. Once we have all that down, he continues with a chuckle, we can begin to help others do the same whereby sharing our own unique gifts and graces with our brothers and sisters.

Padre has a great joy about his being because he knows he is a Beloved and loved Child of God. He does not wonder anymore. He knows that God is for him, not against him. Great teachers, as he is, share this "Good News" with those who seek it. We are not here to keep the jewels and gems we have learned and experienced to ourselves. It is our Spiritual Responsibility to lay it out for all to hear. With a heart full of Gratitude, I Celebrate Padre Paul and honor him for his selfless work with humanity.

Most of CLM's bi-yearly four-day retreats had been held in Illinois until 2014. At that time, and for the next couple of years, one retreat was held in New Jersey and the other in California. We had begun and continued to merge with Dana's School, the Foundation for Spiritual Development. Many of his students and teachers began attending these retreats. While I know we all had our growing pains with this merging and our own unique needs for Spiritual Growth, I can honestly state that we have all become a beautiful and loving family. CLM presently holds both retreats in California. During these retreats, if one is remaining open, or even has a mustard seed of faith, as Ron Roth used to say, "all the angels will swoop in with comfort and grace on your behalf."

Padre Paul and his team, Dana and Bobee, along with a couple of guest speakers that Padre chooses from our Monk and Ordained community, give PowerPoint and Pictorial Presentations. These presentations share Truth, Wisdom, Grace and Holy Moments that move through their energy fields. These presentations and Healing Services have resulted in a number of participants testifying to both emotional and physical healings. Guided meditations, poems, and prayers are recited by community members throughout the four days of the retreat.

Music is an important piece of our healing retreats. Many songs of high vibrational frequencies are played as the day begins, before each new session, and as we spiritually prepare our own Holy Temples to receive the Holy Grace that awaits us. As we sing and rejoice, the atmosphere changes. The energy in the room shifts lighter as we enter into our Beloved's Embrace! It is an experience to behold. For those who are interested in learning more about CLM you can visit their website at www. CelebratingLifeMinistries.com

I will end this chapter with a favorite prayer of mine by the late Ron Roth.

> *Infinite Creator of the Cosmos, Mother of all life, my greatest intention is to feel the vital breath of your healing Spirit upon me, driving from me all the fog that has obscured my vision in the past. My greatest hope, my greatest desire, my greatest intention right now is to come fully into your healing presence with an awareness of all your magnificence saturating me, surrounding me and bathing everything with light. Thank you, God, for being so faithful and sure to your promises.*

Chapter 10

Growing and Evolving in Ministry

In September 2015 we invited Padre Paul to visit Connecticut from his home in Illinois, to facilitate a Healing Service at a nearby Unity Church that my Dad and I were part of at that time. We also planned on having Padre host private healing sessions with people during his visit.

Ahead of his visit I had been invited to share some teachings of Ron Roth each Sunday morning over the course of four weeks at the Unity Church. The timing was perfect, as although my father and I had spoken of Ron, Paul and Celebrating Life Ministries to some of our friends, and other congregants at the church; actually sharing teachings and video were the perfect segway ahead of Padre Paul's visit.

One important piece with CLM's Healing Services, is the way in which people receive healing. I have shared with readers how this works in my first book, and I took the opportunity during the classes I facilitated to explain what "resting in the Spirit" meant. I was very impressed with how so many of the congregants were open to this when the time actually came for Padre's visit. One undertaking that my Dad and I needed to do before Padre's visit was to train a few men, and we even had one woman, to learn how to safely "catch" someone and ease them to the carpeted floor, so that they could safely "rest in the Spirit." I had volunteers' practice with me and they all picked up on the process very quickly.

Before I knew it, the time had finally arrived for Padre Paul's visit and our Healing Service; it flowed so beautifully. Padre invited a couple of CLM community members, that had attended from neighboring states, to share stories of healing at the beginning of our service. He spoke to the congregation about being open and receptive to the healing that we are in need of and desire. Prayers and a meditation were offered as well. During the healing portion of the Service, many people did in fact "rest in the Spirit." It was a wonderful day of Healing and Grace!

Padre made a return visit to Connecticut in April of 2016. As last time, Padre had Private Healing Sessions with people. On Sunday afternoon after Unity's regular service, he facilitated another Healing Service. This time people were more familiar with the process and flow. Many hearts were opened and healed in this Spirit led event. We all rejoiced with Great Gratitude!

Little did I know what was in store for me after the Healing Service we held. The next day Padre and I had a conversation about the joy we felt with the receptivity from people at the service. He then looked at me and said, "You know, Shari, I have answered the call to light the fire here and it is up to you to keep it going." My first reaction was a bit of terror for the unfamiliar. As I later sat in meditation with his statement, however, the guidance showed up in a very clear way and it became obvious that this was the next step in my journey.

I had been facilitating Healing Services at Unity for several years. The big difference between what Padre Paul was suggesting and what I had previously done was that I had people sit in chairs to receive their healing. The idea of having congregants stand to receive Healing and asking for volunteer catchers was a BIG step for me. This was going to involve more responsibility on my part; a much deeper surrender to the outcome and a complete trust in the process. I knew, however, that if the Divine wanted me to step into this role, I could only say YES!

Through meditation I received guidance to begin with this change for people to receive healing at my next service in June. I was fortunate enough to have the commitment of two dear friends to be catchers for these services, which took place every other month. Before I knew it, the day of the service had arrived. I explained to attendees that they would be standing to receive healing, and I reviewed the idea of "resting in the Spirit" if they felt touched by the Spirit to do so. I pointed out the catchers who would be behind them and they should not worry about free falling.

I also reassured attendees that those who, for whatever reason, could not stand or were concerned about this new way of Healing would be ushered to chairs set aside by my friend Deborah for healing. Deborah beautifully decorated the altars with simple elegance ahead of the service.

After a poem shared by my Dad, from his book of poetry, my message, prayer and meditation, it was time for the Healing portion of the service. It was a sight to behold as everyone was open to what was aligned for them to receive. My dad walked before each person to Bless them with Holy Rose Oil. After that I made my way along the diagonal line of people, reading the hearts of each that were being channeled through me. While I had been used by the Holy Spirit in this way for quite some time in services and private sessions with clients, this service was different. There was a deliberate flow of certainty that came out of my mouth. I could feel my angels and guides working on behalf of all those present. My egoic mind was set aside in the delivery of messages uniquely created for each person. I moved among all with a sense of ease and inner wisdom that I had not expected for this first service. A confidence that was otherworldly emanated forth from me.

It was not until the end of the service, when I personally was feeling a bit woozy from the intervention of the Spirit world, that my father told me all, but one person, had rested in the Spirit. I felt astonished, as I was still feeling a bit surprised to be facilitating healing in this way. I will say, at the same time though, I felt I had come home. It felt glorious to be called for service in this deeper and Sacred way!

It feels the perfect time now to share with you this piece written by Susi Roos in her book *The Divine Dance.*

> *I offer this day to you Spirit to use as you would for through you, I come alive and through me you live. I offer your Grace to the world with compassion non-judgment and love, and in this moment know that forgiveness is only needed when we forget who we truly are.*
>
> *So, I offer it to myself as your vehicle to see and give only love. Guide me so I may rise above fear-based thoughts. I surrender my life, my purpose, and all my vestments to you, knowing that in doing so, Faith reigns and I express with*

> *love, joy, and serving intention.*
> *Ahmeyn.*

I was guided some months later, that in addition to these daytime bi-monthly services, it would be well received if I planned a few Candlelight Healing Services throughout the year, to be held on Saturday evenings. I have always felt as though I were a child of the night, and the glow of candlelight holds a vibrational glory of its own. My friend Lee supported me at each one, by holding Sacred Energy and many event logistics ahead of these services. The first was held in December 2016. It was a very Sacred and Holy time for all of us. The candlelight stirred the magic and Fire of Healing Energy all about the Sanctuary. We all expressed that this was the start of deeper and more profound encounters with the Divine. I continued with day and evening services at Unity Church for the next few years.

After many years of Healing Services at this Unity Church, I received guidance that it was time for me to move on, providing services elsewhere. I was fortunate enough to be invited by another Unity Minister, Reverend Carolyn, to facilitate Spirit-Led Healing Services at the

Unity Church where she presides. This offer filled me with excitement and gratitude for this new and wonderous opportunity! Reverend Carolyn is a medium as well as a Minister, therefore her vibration and intuition was in sync with the work I am called to facilitate.

Additionally, many congregants at this church were open and receptive to healing and balance. Reverend Carolyn holds the umbrella of Love, Unity and Oneness with her community; and all people there support one another with their own unique gifts of service. It has been a beautiful expression within this church for me to witness and be a part of! I am grateful that my dear friend Jim continued acting as catcher for the bi-monthly Healing Services in Torrington. We had some people from the other Unity church where I had been, attend healing services here as well. My Dad continued to share one of his poems and Blessed participants with Rose Oil. My sweet friend Cheryl joined us by giving her Sacred Service touch to our altar, for these Healing Services at Unity in the Foothills.

I am grateful for the Guidance and Spiritual Growth I have experienced with facilitating these Healing Services, and I continue to flourish in service with Celebrating Life Ministries. Padre

Paul came back to Connecticut in 2017, and together we led a beautiful Healing event in my home. We had fifty attendees which was the most we could fit comfortably in our downstairs, where all could see. Padre and I both shared a message of positive intention with everyone. We then shared prayers and a meditation as well. During the healing portion of the service we moved chairs out of the way and placed yoga mats on my hard wood floors. Padre had the wonderful idea of giving people a choice to receive their healing outside in my backyard surrounded by nature. Blankets were laid in a circle on the grass for the possibility of "resting in the Spirit." Padre led and I assisted him with healings. It was a glorious sunny September day of about eighty degrees. Some people chose to receive their healing inside, either in a chair, or standing with a yoga mat for them to rest upon. We had three catchers, two Jim's and my son Ryan.

After all the healings were received by Holy Spirit, my backyard was a glorious site to behold. A circle of sisters and brothers Resting in Spirit in a circle of Unity and Oneness. We were and are so grateful for our CLM friends from neighboring states, combined with some of my friends from Unity, who came to help with registration, coordinating the music CD's, etc... and providing an overall supportive energy and vibration! Thinking back on this event brings great joy to my heart and soul!

Padre Paul and one of his team members, Dana, came to Connecticut from California to facilitate these two-day events once a year over the next two years; 2018 and 2019. They became known as East of Heaven Healing Events; the East part is, of course, because these took place on the east coast. As the events grew, we decided to have them in a hotel as my home would not have been large enough to accommodate the increased number of people that we were anticipating.

The undertaking and planning with a hotel, was a whole new learning and growth experience for me. It was decided to have the East of Heaven events on a Friday evening for a few hours, then all day on Saturday. Some people would be driving from neighboring states and others would be flying in. Many would need to book a hotel room for a one or two-night stay to attend these sessions. I worked with a hotel local to the nearby airport regarding the number of rooms, pricing, meal options for

Saturday lunch, a water station just for our group, number of tables and chairs needed, etc. Boy did I learn a lot. I was also given the privilege and honor, by Padre's invitation, to give a PowerPoint presentation at each of the 2018 and 2019 East of Heaven Healing Events.

I trust that Presence walks with and encourages me every step of the way. As opportunities continue presenting themselves, I shall, with abiding Faith and Courage, say YES to this Spirit Led Work. I am filled in my being with gratitude for everything in my life. It all helps me continue moving forward with un-abiding Faith and Courage.

Chapter 11

Our Power to Heal

Everything is possible when we look to the light within. We are co-creators, and co-healers with the source of our being. Know this truth, practice this truth, be/live this truth and it will set you free! We are part of every process. One of my most profound teachers, the late Ron Roth, used to say, "We need to know that we have the Power and Authority to DECLARE whatever we desire."

At times along the way of life, however, we get stuck and lose our way; we may even believe that we don't have this power, but some others do. This makes me think of the Nursery Rhyme statement "Not I said the little Red Hen." I say, if not you, then why not? Do you think of yourself as less than, not worthy of, not smart enough?

These are interesting observations that may be coming from your egoic mind and are most certainly not coming from Creator. I would like to share with you, my personal history and what I overcame to arrive where I am today.

I grew up challenged academically. I struggled in school with grades and could not stay focused on schoolwork and tests. Back in the 60's and 70's, this condition was not diagnosed or addressed. I became aware, as an adult, that I had some Attention Deficit Disorder. I still deal with this in my life for certain situations, but I know now how to help myself through the process. I am a good listener with the Source of my being, who is always there to assist me and all of us when we open ourselves up. As a child I did struggle with feelings of not being smart enough. These thoughts lead to feelings of not being good enough and an overall feeling of being unworthy. Having two loving parents who never judged or belittled me for any seeming shortcomings, was my saving grace. Also, through my inner listening to Holy Spirit's advice, I have healed and learned how to quiet my mind to read slowly and comprehend, mitigating my Attention Deficit Disorder. I can now be very organized and orderly when it is needed. These are two difficulties I had to deal with growing up.

I am very grateful that I had the privilege, the willingness, and courage to cocreate my healing in these areas. Those of us who are aware of the power to create, that lies within our being, can sometimes feel fearful with possessing this Spiritual ability.

We literally can become afraid of "ourselves," whereby dimming this inner light. In doing so, we deny our Spiritual Responsibility with Sacred Service for Humanity. I implore you as I have done, to rise above these lower thoughts, and trust the wisdom of truth from the still small voice that lights our way.

I can certainly confess that at times throughout my life I have had these feelings. Aside from minor setbacks, due to life and circumstances, I now feel strong, courageous and fearless. I know that I am never alone. My Beloved Divine Presence, Angels and Spirit Guide team are by my side always! I call upon them regularly for assistance and stay tapped in with higher vibration to hear what they wish to share with me.

Joel Osteen, whom some of you may be familiar with, is an Evangelical Preacher in

Houston, Texas. I am pursuing a Spiritual Life, as does Joel, but I do not share the organized Religious piece of his faith. That being said, I have great admiration for him, and his conviction with helping others to empower themselves. Joel has shared a story with his congregation a number of times, and I will share it here with you. This is a particular story about his mother and her faith during a time that would break most of us.

Joel's mother was diagnosed with liver cancer when she was just forty-five years old, and still had the responsibility of raising five children. Her diagnosis was grim, and doctors gave her three months to live. Of course, she was fearful but according to Joel, only at first. By an act of the will she chose not to put her focus on fear, worry or concern for her family. She declared that her diagnosis would not control her destiny, but that it was between her and God. She instead set out to help people who were, as she felt, worse off than she was. Her Faith led the way. She displayed incredible strength, courage, and devotion to helping others in greater need than her own; something many would not have the fortitude to face. The outcome from this experience is that she received miraculous Healing. I watched Joel giving this testimony on a televised service. At the time his mother was still alive and, in her eighties, and was sitting in the front row listening to Joel's story.

A few years ago, after I watched Joel share this story on television, my daughter, Holly, and I took a long weekend trip to Houston, where I was born. We stopped by the home that I lived in with my family while on this visit so I could share my personal history with her. Since she and I were staying right near Lakewood, where Joel Osteen holds his services, we attended one on the Sunday we were there. With us being out of towners, ushers brought us right up to the third row. The service was musical, lively, funny and very inspiring. I am grateful for the opportunity of attending in person and for the honor of meeting Joel and being able to compliment him for his service to humanity.

The story Joel shared about his mother brings to mind what Paramhansa Yogananda, yogi and master teacher, said; that when you can control your own destiny, by your willpower, you can do tremendous things. As you can see, the story about Joel's mother is a delightful example of doing just this. Stories such as this remind me of what Gandhi said "In a gentle way you can shake the world. To give pleasure to a single heart by a single act is better than a thousand heads bowing in prayer."

Many Master Teachers have encouraged us to "wake up," stop making excuses and ignite "our power to heal." One such Master Teacher was Jesus, who in essence, still assists us today. He proclaimed for all who had ears to hear, "You will do as I have done, and greater things than these shall you do." When speaking to the people of his time, he ended that statement with "because I go to the Father." He was speaking of the power within each and every one of us at the core of our being. There are many names that are used by people individually, when addressing, this presence and power. Whatever name feels aligned for you is perfect. It's having a relationship and connection with this presence that matters. I shall end this chapter with a lovely piece written by Susi Roos in her book *The Divine Dance*. This depicts the Spirit within, speaking to us.

> *Reach for my presence wherever you are, in the midst of any and every activity. Listen to my voice*

whispering in every interaction and ego dominated experience.

I am the light and the way, illuminating as brightly as you would allow. Never are you alone, never are you left to your own devices, unless you choose to shut off my voice. For I will never shout. Lift your voice in chorus with mine, and the world will hear you sing, through your senses, which calibrate vibratory rate.

Lift your vibratory rate and expand your vision to see the abundance of love and beauty beyond this physical dimension. Seek time to experience this true reality each day, and you will begin to live in a new way, fully loving and accepting your own magnificence, and the magnificence of all brothers and sisters.

Ahmeyn

Chapter 12

Graciously Grateful

Dee Wallace, in her book *Conscious Creation*, stated that "when you are filled with gratitude and awe for life you are vibrating at a higher frequency. While gratitude is a place of centered living, being grateful also has overall health benefits for our body, mind, and spirit. Being Grateful and having Gratitude is a choice, just like everything else."

Celebrating Life Ministries proclaims the statement "Thank you God for Everything." You may be thinking "are you crazy?!" Or that there is no way I am going to be grateful for lousy relationships, little money, poor health, loneliness, anxiety, etc. First of all, just like everything else it can begin with "I want to like..." or "I want to be grateful that I lost my job." Although you may not know the reason this may have happened, or maybe you do, there is a spiritual reason behind it all. It could be that the job was not aligned for you anymore, and if you chose to be grateful, or to begin with wanting to be grateful, chose to acknowledge that there is something else better for you, your vibration and frequency will go up. This then can align with Universal Energy for a favorable outcome.

At the same time, it is important to work on forgiving, if needed, any people involved in your present situation, including yourself. In this example, it may be your boss, coworkers, or others that had a hand in your being let go from your job. This can feel like a harsh reality, and difficult for you to process, especially if you may be feeling like "a victim." Please hear me when I say, there are no victims. This too is only a choice that comes from free will and will have unfavorable and negative consequences for you, should you embrace it. It is best to never take the word "victim" into your consciousness. Instead, take a breath, pause, and allow feelings of gratitude for all that is going well in your life to come forward.

If you are feeling there is nothing to feel

grateful for at present, then begin with the Blessing it is that you can breathe. For without this you would have no life. Next, if you have food to eat and water to drink, then your body and entire physical being are being sustained. Breath, food, and water are the things that many of us possess and can be grateful for. This is a great place to start. By holding an attitude of gratitude, for even just these building blocks of life, along with the path of forgiveness I mentioned earlier, your vibration will find the balance that is needed for you to move forward in Grace.

When I think back on my life with some of the intense challenges, and spiritual growth lessons that I have endured, I can actually see the Blessing in all of them. As I have grown in the process of trusting that there is Universal Divine Order, I am now able to move through these lessons when they arise, feeling the Blessings and Grace as they are occurring, despite the initial hardships they bring. I have great trust that everything is manifesting for my highest truth and evolutionary process. My faith helps me accept this for everyone and trust in "soul balance" as a major component with the unfolding process that is life.

Dee Wallace reminds us that we are never failures. We are successfully experiencing our process of reawakening. And, of course, the process is different for all of us. The last point she makes is, to be filled with the experience of gratitude, is when we authentically know we are creation itself.

In my first book, *Living in Grace*, the statement I made regarding "Grace" is as follows:

> *Grace is a "state of being," an awareness of "I am Spirit, Divine, whole, and complete in this present moment and always." Whatever may be happening with or around us – Grace affords us the ability to see things in a new light. To possibly change our perspective and paradigm. To see through the eyes of creator, the order and perfection in all things.*

I still embrace that statement of Grace that I wrote six years ago. I am concluding this chapter with three prayers by Yogananda. I have recited these prayers together as though they were one, at many of my Spirit Led Healing Services. Their flow together unites harmoniously.

Oh Spirit, make my Soul thy temple but make my heart thy beloved home where thou may dwell with me in ease and everlasting understanding.

Divine Mother with the language of my soul, I ask realization of thy presence. Thou art the essence of everything. Make me see thee with every fiber of my being. With every wisp of thought awaken my heart.

Oh, bestower of unceasing bliss, I will seek to make others truly happy in Gratitude for the Divine Joy thou hast given me. Through my Spiritual Happiness I will serve all.

Chapter 13

Our Global Pandemic

I have been given guidance to write this chapter for all of us living now, and for others who may read my thoughts on the Pandemic in generations to come. As 2020 unfolded our world began experiencing a Global Viral Pandemic that has been called SARS-COV-2 or COVID19. This virus is said to have originated in China, but it has not been definitively proven how it transmuted to be spread by humans. Speculation has suggested it may have begun at a wet market, a place where exotic animals are brought in raised and sold, by a worker who was been bitten by a bat infected with the virus. Another theory is that scientists in China may have been working with this virus in a lab setting infecting one of the employees who then infected others in the area. At any rate, it did originate in Wuhan China before spreading across the globe.

This is a highly contagious virus that is transmitted by breath, coughing, sneezing and surface touching. The feeling is that it can lay dormant on countertops and other surfaces, cardboard boxes, packages, mail, groceries, for a period of time. If one's fingertips touches any of these surfaces it can then be transmitted when one touches their nose, eyes or mouth through the membranes in these areas.

COVID-19 is a respiratory virus. People with underlying health conditions such as high blood pressure, diabetes, or other underlying immune suppressed conditions, along with the elderly are the most vulnerable if they contract this virus. In some people the virus has also caused problems with not just one's lungs, which is the respiratory aspect of the virus, but also other organs throughout the body.

The United States has been dealing with the virus for the past six months. As I stated earlier, it originated in China where it spread from person to person before making its way to Europe. In late February, President Trump closed Chinese travel to the United States expecting that this would keep the pandemic from spreading into our country. Unfortunately, the virus had spread to Europe and travelers were still flowing into the United States, which is likely how the virus began to be widely transmitted throughout the country and the rest of the world. All this being said, life as we knew it changed across the entire globe. The changes we have had to make because of this virus has caused humanity to create a new normal.

Medical experts and scientists gave the guidance for people throughout the United States to quarantine for two weeks; the time it takes for the virus to no longer be contagious. There was a mass shut down of all non-essential business, schools, travel, etc. In states and countries where governments took this guidance seriously there was an impact on the virus spread. Locations that did not quarantine did not see the spread of this disease diminish. The end result of a global quarantine was that many people were furloughed or fired form their jobs. As bills could not be paid by owners, businesses scaled down, and people feared working would increase their chance of contracting the virus due to underlying health conditions.

A Corona Virus task force was put into place at the start. Initially, the recommendation from government agencies was for people to social distance, keeping at least six feet apart from one another and washing of one's hands for twenty seconds after touching surfaces. As the pandemic progressed wearing masks in public places, such as grocery stores, was mandated and in other places the recommendation was to wear masks. Over the past few months, businesses have slowly been reopening, while the recommendation for people to wear a mask and social distance has not been lifted. Vaccines for Covid-19 are being worked on, and scientists are hopeful that after the trials are complete people will be able to individually get one over the next six months or so.

Our country is also experiencing an uprising over systemic racism which began after a black man was killed by a police officer. What spawned from this were protestors in the city where this event occurred which has led to protests in other cities. Initially protests began peacefully before others joined in with violent acts of rioting and looting. This has gone on for a few months now, and in the midst of it all, at least two more black men were shot by police. These shootings were unrelated to the protesting and riots. One of these men died, and the other is paralyzed. So much fear has been circulating in the world since the Pandemic began. We have had five and a half million Corona Virus cases as of this writing and one hundred and eighty thousand deaths in the United States. Many people have lost loved ones or friends to the virus. Our economy has suffered greatly with businesses closing or scaling way back, job loss, etc.

Every individual has had their own hardships and changes to deal with throughout this Pandemic. Many have been and are suffering and feeling challenged in ways of emotional, spiritual and or physical imbalances as well. I, myself, have had my own healings and lessons to learn over the past six months. Before I speak about some of these challenges, I would like to share an Aramaic version of the Lord's Prayer. Many of the words in this prayer reflect the importance of what we personally need and what our world desperately needs at this time.

> *Father – Mother! Birther and*
> *Breath of All. Create a space inside*
> *us and fill it with your presence.*
> *Let oneness now prevail. Your one*

desire then acts through Ours, as energy fills all forms. Give us physical and spiritual nourishment each day. Untangle the knots of error that bind us as we release others. Don't let appearances make us forgetful of the source, but free us to act appropriately. Age to Age from you comes the Glorious harmony of Life. May these statements be fertile ground from which our future grows.

Ahmeyn

When I first received the news that the Pandemic Virus, Covid19, was beginning to spread in our country I felt fear. This fear was not only for myself but also for my family. Both of my parents are older, and mom is immune compromised. I began watching too much of the news on television and my vibration began to lower. Although I was continuing to meditate and have some prayer time each morning, I was too engaged in the negativity of broadcast news. Unfortunately, I did not immediately realize this fact. It was not until I noticed that I was starting to become edgy. I was being 'triggered' by all of the unfolding circumstances and events of the Pandemic combined with Systemic Racism. These 'triggers' brought up beliefs and patterns, that had been held with very deep rigidity, in my consciousness from childhood. They were learned from religious views of right and wrong, good and bad. The time came when I needed to step away from the daily reporting of the virus and its effects on the world. Sometimes I would ask my husband, Bob, what the latest updates were, so I did not have to sit and listen to the television myself. As I began changing the habit and pattern that I had formed with the daily news briefings from the media and the President, peace began to be restored within my being. This, of course, was just in time as there were other lessons on the horizon for me.

With everyone social distancing, churches were no longer meeting in person. Many services were, and still are, being broadcast via Facebook or Zoom. I, therefore, would no longer be facilitating Healing Services at Unity in the Foothills in person since Sunday morning Services would no longer be taking place. This felt like a big loss for me, as the work of Spirit that I am called to do is a very important part of my life. It fulfills my Soul and purpose. Now, with what felt like the blink of an eye, it would no longer be; for who knows how long. I really needed to sit and be with my feelings around what my Spirit-Led work would look like now as I could not imagine another way of facilitating this work.

As I sat with my emotions, the wisdom that came to mind was that a new way will open up. It is okay to let that old way go for even if it may not come around again, I felt a great sense of calm, peace and acceptance all about my being. I realized that I had become "attached" to this piece of my work. It is never healthy to be attached to anything or anyone of this world for everything and everyone here is and are fleeting. Nothing is permanent. While it is wonderful to love and be loving of others and things, we must express with loving nonattachment.

It is very important for me to mention here, before I move forward with sharing how the pandemic has affected me, I am one of the fortunate ones. I did not lose my job; I have not lost a relative or friend to the virus and I have not had the virus myself. I am very grateful for all of this!

As the Quarantine began in mid-March, I received the guidance that, although I would not continue facilitating Healing Services at Unity in the Foothills, another way would be revealed to me. At times, I am able to continue to tune in with Reverend Carolyn and the congregation via Zoom. It is truly a treat to be able to stay connected with the friends I have made there in this way. Prior to the Pandemic starting, Zoom was just beginning to gain popularity as a way for people to stay in touch with one another and for people to host events. The Pandemic escalated the adoption of this technology for all. My son, Ryan, shared screens with me through Skype, teaching me how to use Zoom. I facilitated my first Zoom Healing Session on April 4th. It has been well received and I have continued doing so since then. These monthly sessions consist of me sharing a brief message of positive intention, prayer, brief guided meditation followed by Healing Decrees. I feel so Blessed for this Sacred and Holy time with those who tune in.

I have mentioned in previous chapters that I am part of Celebrating Life Ministries. I was to have attended a four-day CLM Healing Retreat in California this past April. With the Pandemic spreading throughout the United States in March this retreat had to be cancelled. While I fully trusted that this process was for all of our safety, I also had a piece of sadness that came up for me. I needed to "be" with my emotional feelings of missing my spiritual family and not being able to give Sacred Service with those who would attend. There was certainly a piece of grieving that I allowed my being to move through. I also needed to accept the unknown that was in the mix as well. Not knowing when we would all be able to gather safely again weighed heavily on me. As I sat in meditation with my Beloved Divine Presence, I was reminded, as I am from time to time, that all is in order for all of us. From here I felt a great sense of peace and balance come over me. These words came to mind for myself and my loving CLM community, we will meet again when and if it is aligned. With that, I gave up any control, fear or restrictions I may have been holding surrounding this outcome.

I am very grateful that CLM has been facilitating a three part Zoom series each month that helps me stay centered and connected with this community. They initially began in April with Padre Paul, Dana and Bobee leading online services for the first three months of the pandemic. After that, Padre has invited two people from his community of Monks and Ordained members to co-facilitate with him for each of these series. I was honored to be one of the co-facilitators with him for the July three part series. It is very spiritually fulfilling for me to continue teaching and sharing Sacred Service. I am grateful for all aligned opportunities in which to BE the light that humanity greatly needs at present.

The one thing that most of us have had some fear around, at certain points during this Pandemic, is the "unknown" of when the virus may truly soften enough for people not to wear masks for safety and to ease social distancing measures in place. Many of us feel that we have moved into a "new normal" and that many ways of being and living will never return to the way they were before the Pandemic. This pandemic has been an opportunity for us all to stretch our ability to comprehend, process and metabolize into our consciousness "attachment healing." We can never be so attached to "our life," this includes all aspects of it, that we cannot accept change whether we have made a conscious decision for it or it is brought upon us as part of the collective. Not being attached is part of a deeper level of understanding that awaits us all!

It is often not easy to accept these changes with grace. I am continuing my process with doing so, and I hope you will as well.

We must remain hopeful especially during these times of seeming unrest. I will share with you now some words I have written for comfort, balance, and peace that you may be seeking at this time. May you feel and allow these words to penetrate your very being, refreshing and restoring all aspects of your existence.

> *It is time to walk in a new way with one another, on this plane we call Earth. We have the opportunity to awaken, grow in consciousness, and embrace our destiny.*
>
> *Let us forgive and release our past misfortunes, while holding space for others to do so as well. Together we can choose to fully surrender every part of our being, allowing Divine Healing for ourselves, past generations, and those yet to come. May we be restored to the state of Glory and Illumination.*

Help me Beloved Creator to Grace each person I meet, all events and circumstances, with the same Love and respect that I have for myself. I am grateful to move forward with my brothers and sisters of every faith and color, towards full equality in all things.

As we stand for ONE in Unity, evolution unfolds before our eyes, and our destinies' pave the way for the future of humanity's unfolding process.

And so, it is,

AHMEYN

Chapter 14

From Fear to Faith

When I think back through my life, I have had countless times when I have been in a state of fear. Sometimes fearful or fear-based thoughts seemed to show up out of nowhere that I could readily identify. Often during these occurrences, I would feel very confused as though I were lost and alone. Looking back and observing some of my fears, that stand out for me as an adult, I see a common lesson in all of them which I shall share here and then write a bit more about later in this chapter.

As I shared in my first book, I was moving through a serious health challenge of Level Three Cervical Dysplasia in 1998. My first reaction to this diagnosis was feeling "scared to death." A great fear and darkness came over me and I experienced, possibly, the most heightened terror of my life. I feared the idea of possibly dying and leaving my children to grow up without their mother. It wasn't until I literally dropped to the floor on my back sobbing like a child, arms outstretched in surrender that I began to hear a voice of guidance. In that moment of calm, I was shown what needed to be done and experienced in order for me to once again be well and whole. The most important action I could take for full recovery would be prayer and meditation; making an effort to commune with Creator. This was a huge piece of my healing.

After 9/11, September 11, 2001, I felt very vulnerable, and dipped into great fear from the Terrorist attacks in our country. My two children were both in Middle School at that time. I vividly remember picking them up from school that afternoon. The school had only told students that something happened in our country and that each child's parents would explain the situation to them. I remember telling my kids by myself what happened that afternoon as their father was still at work. While my children seemed to handle the news with sadness, they felt reassured by my words that they were safe. I, however, was not being honest with them about how I truly felt.

I took on a consciousness of fear and did not feel safe in my day to day living. I developed a bit of paranoia if I passed by someone whom I may have thought to be a terrorist. I had concerns that there could be pockets of people around that could infiltrate into towns and possibly harm my family and others. I was afraid to fly on an airplane and did not do so for at least two years afterwards. I had forgotten the peace and joy of my relationship with Creator. You see, we all can forget. As the saying goes, sometimes people flock to Creator in times of need, but often move away from this relationship once things become balanced again.

During the three years between the terrorist attacks in 2001 and when I felt the call to Celebrating Life Ministries in 2004, I felt okay at best with the emotional part of my life at that time. Some of the initial fears of additional terrorist attacks after 9/11 had subsided. In 2003 I had finally flown on a plane again but felt fear for the entire flight. By the summer and then the Fall of 2003, I was feeling desperate for "more" in my life. I have always been a joyful, enthusiastic person, but I now seemed to be running low on my zest for life. It turns out that something was going on with my Kidney as well. Looking back, this now makes me think of the television series Lost in Space from the 1970's. I vividly recall "Robot" with flailing arms and lights flashing, exclaiming "Danger Will Robinson." I was personally now being "alerted" that turbulent waters were again beginning to churn. Why is it that for some, as with me, the processes of unrest needs to be repeated? While many of us know there are a variety of reasons for our experiences. My Faith tells me that all these reasons boil down to our souls yearning to be in relationship with the Source of our being.

While attending my first retreat with CLM in 2004, I was "born again in the Spirit." I had been made aware (remembered) that I am a Beloved Child of Divine Presence. I knew in the instant I first felt and experienced this truth that my life had been renewed. My life force improved, and I would never be the same. My Beloved was with me 24/7, and I could never go back to hopeless feelings again. I flew home from this retreat feeling fearless of the plane and have not been afraid to fly ever since. This does not mean, however, that I have not had more learning experiences, and moments of forgetting as I certainly have. We are all still living in Human Form as well as Spirit. Having a foundation with Creator and a daily growing relationship through continued awareness, along with meditation/prayer, I am able to tap back into my inner knowing, raise my vibration and realign in Faith.

Hafiz, a well-known poet who lauded the joys of love, said: "I wish I could show you when you are feeling lonely or in darkness, the astonishing light of your own beauty." What a transformative and truthful statement.

In 2006, I felt the call to begin facilitating Healing Services. My passion to do so was very strong, however, it would involve public speaking to a group of people. Fear came up for me surrounding this issue. You see I had forgotten who I was. I was thinking it would be "Shari" the human-ego me that would be talking. I placed my own apprehensive feelings of "what if my talk isn't good enough, what if they simply don't like what I am saying" aside. I began these services anyway, as I was listening to my inner guidance from the Divine and my Spiritual Team. It was literally a few years, before I FINALLY gave the "speaking" part to

Creator. This allowed me to "hear" more clearly what I was to say. As I did so, the thoughts of "will people like what I am saying" went right out the door. I no longer cared. I knew the message was from the one who knows all, and if others don't like it, that is their issue to deal with. A huge weight was lifted after this, and the flow of the services was and has continued to be beautiful.

I shared in the previous chapter about the Global Pandemic that we are in the midst of, and a bit about the Racial Unrest in the United States. A few months into the Pandemic a black man, named George Floyd, was murdered by a white Police Officer who kept his knee on the man's neck until he could no longer enter a breath. Even after this man had no pulse, the officer kept his knee there for extra minutes.

While I had found a more level place in my consciousness, releasing many fears surrounding all the changes occurring with the Pandemic, this horrific situation brought about a setback for me. I allowed myself to feel anger, and very deep sorrow for several days. I began to judge and condemn all those involved in this horrific incident. I was being triggered by deeply rooted rigidity (as I mentioned in Chapter 13) in my subconscious since childhood (surrounding my religions teachings). This rigidity was with regard to good/bad, right/wrong. Often, at some point in our life, these beliefs/patterns that may have laid dormant come to the surface for healing. As this process unfolded, I was also beginning to experience an acute health imbalance as my vibration was plummeting. The great Blessing in this situation was that I became aware that I was not staying aligned with Creator vibration. Although I was making connection with the Divine through meditation each day, I had not stayed mindful to be in this space throughout my days. All of this boiled down to one word: FEAR. It was when I "woke up" from the fog that had obscured my vision of flow, that I returned to my deep Trust and Faith that all things are in Divine Order. We don't need to understand why, if we walk by Faith – not by Sight. Some may feel this is "blind" faith and reckless behavior. I share with you now, that this Faith has literally and metaphorically saved my life on many occasions. I then was able to hold compassion for George and his family, but I let the fear go.

My guidance in all of this is the same as it was with flying on planes, the Cervical

Dysplasia, Public Speaking, this Pandemic and all other FEARS I have experienced in my life... SEEK FIRST THE KINGDOM. This may sound preachy or Bible Based, but what it means is seek the indwelling Presence – the Spirit of your being to be your best friend. When fear comes up it is because we feel separated from our natural state – oneness with the source of our being. We can feel scared if we think we are navigating our life alone. Instead make Creator your most trusted confidant. This is the most treasured intimate relationship and union of your life. Having this Presence by your side shows you only Love, Faith and that Fear is but an illusion. When you make the commitment to live in Faith you may have minor setbacks, as we all do, but even in these you will never go down in defeat again; because of your Sacred Union with your Beloved. This is the Promise. I will close this chapter with the beautiful Blessing below. Neil Douglas-Klotz, a scholar in religious studies and spirituality, expanded the following Biblical Blessing from the Qumran community of the Dead Sea, written between 100BC and AD100. Neil says this is a Blessing of Lucid Fire and Secret Grace.

May the being of the Universe breathe into you the light of Blessing and Ripeness, the fulfillment of health and balance; may it protect you from distractions brittle and bent with a sphere of Lucid Fire. May it enlighten the heart of your passions with the contemplation of Living Energy. May it uncover the hidden strength within you, insight gathered from the external now. And may it show you its face of Secret Grace and silent refuge in a communion of deep peace.

AHMEYN

Chapter 15

Become the Miraculous

In his book, "Miracles," Stuart Wilde invokes a phrase that acknowledges the Miraculous within each and every one of us. He writes "I am <u>Eternal, Immortal, Universal</u> and <u>Infinite.</u> What I am is beautiful." Those of us on a Spiritual journey in this life know the aforementioned statement to be truth. We can repeat these truths of our being every day, embrace them with feeling into our consciousness and BE THE MIRACULOUS. Every present moment counts, so let's get to work.

When we were children many of us believed we were invincible. We may have frolicked throughout our days with a carefree innocence, unbridled by concern or worry. Our play may have been imaginative, creative, light and airy.

As we watched butterflies and birds fly about with ease and grace our beings were attuned with this order of purity. We may have gazed at the moon and stars, yearning to get closer to visit their mysteries.

When my son, Ryan, was growing up he was fascinated by the moon. Ryan and his sister, Holly, loved teetertottering together on our swing set. His imagination would quickly take over as he looked at the sky. He would say "Holly, let's go to the moon." Holly would reply, "I want to go to Disney World!" as that was a favorite family vacation of ours. Ryan would then concede and utter, "Okay, we'll go to Disneyworld first, and then to the moon." He could not let go of the mystery and enchantment that he felt awaited him there. We did go on to buy him a telescope a short time later and he marveled with star gazing.

My daughter Holly loved picking me a bouquet of flowers every day during summertime. The flowers were beautiful yellow dandelions that grew in abundance in our backyard. Although dandelions are labeled as weeds, I have always thought of them as lovely bright yellow sunshines. Holly had a curiosity with daddy long leg spiders. She was fascinated by the length of their legs. When the family would tent camp, if a spider like this got into our sleeping area Holly was the token child to let it out.

As a child, I have very vivid memories of playing house in my neighbor's far backyard. She and I would walk into a wooded area, where the shaded trees cooled down our heat laden little bodies. This place was magical. I felt a sweet delightful presence all around. My friend and I would move the leaves on the ground off to the far sides, so that we could form our woodland homes in the surrounding mounds of dirt. As I touched the dirt with my hands, I felt an indescribable joy and sense of peace. My friend and I each had our own areas that would make up our individual woodland homes. I worked with and molded the dirt to make objects in the rooms of my home. In the kitchen area of my imagined home I would form the dirt to make a table, chairs, sink, and appliances. I had a sleeping room, where I made a bed and dresser. The bathroom had a sink, toilet and bathtub. The final room was filled with a couch, television and coffee table for my family.

While working with my hands in the dirt and feeling attuned to the joyful energies around me, I now realize that this was the presence of fairies. They were communing with me and I with them. We came together in union and love for one another. We were in these present moments together in sync, the "Eternal Now." My memories of this most sacred time in my childhood have helped me attune in deeper ways to all the "aliveness" that surrounds us in nature.

My connection and relationship with nature is the vessel for many of my inspirations and writings that come to life. At this present moment, I am writing this chapter under a tree that borders the backyard woods of my Vermont home. It is a cool fall like day on August 30th. The winds are brisk and there is a chill in the air. As the tree's leaves rustle in the breeze and my hair blows this way and that, the presence of my Beloved pulsates through every cell within me. It ripples with a fluttering sensation and time has stood still. It is in these seeming breathless moments of Illumination that time and space transcend.

What I have just shared is a way of living and being for all of us. Stuart Wilde, a well-known author of self-empowerment and spirituality books, says that "we can give the collective consciousness 'the slip.'" We can choose to break away from the belief of lack and limitations of all kinds that paralyze us in our lives. He says, "we can free and release ourselves from old perceptions and habits." "We can accept a higher vibration of our self."

As I mention in the chapter on our Global Pandemic, we are being given the gift of "slowing down," which is giving us great opportunity and time to be present, regroup and "clean our inner house." It is very helpful to remind ourselves that we are not making these changes alone. We are working with Divine Intelligence. Stuart wrote "There is a 'power' at our disposal that we can use to work Miracles in our lives." This Power is impartial, unemotional and Universal. Stuart calls this power "the Christ mind consciousness."

We all have power within us to be living Miraculous Lives here in this "Heaven on Earth." This feels to be the aligned moment to share with you a meditation, written by Glenda Green in her book, *The Keys of Jeshua.*

> *When you are liberated by silence and no longer involved in the management of life, but in the living of it, you will discover a state*

of awareness in which there is no distraction. Life, itself becomes a prayer. The silence is Prayer and the world of silence in which you are immersed is a baptism of Spirit.

Silence brings enlightenment. Enlightenment brings humility. It is the greatest irony that there is no sense of importance within the glorious, radiant, and loving true self. Only the imaginary self must defend and compare its accomplishment with that of others. That is a vacant reality like one shadow comparing its length with another. In the end, there is no joy in what does not exist. The truest joy, the greatest freedom, is in humility, for in that the heart is rediscovered. This is the source of all good, refreshing the soul as if it were a garden.

We have the glorious opportunity to commune with nature that is all around us. If you live in a city high rise, condominium or apartment you can find nature in a local park.

Nature speaks to us, and we can hear her if we are willing to open ourselves up to her. The animals speak to us as well, just as our domestic furry friends do. This communication has been referred to as telepathic. I see it as spirit to spirt communion. It is a celebration of our oneness with everything. I am sure that many of you have had lovely outdoor animal encounters and possibly communion with them. I'll share a couple of my experiences with you now.

Several years ago, I was walking along my side yard on a warm and sunny summers day. Out of nowhere a Monarch butterfly flew over to me and landed on my bare arm. This had never happened to me before. My arm had been raised from hand to hip level, and this sweet little thing stayed perfectly still as I raised my hand up a little higher. I looked at her feeling so grateful, and I connected spirit to spirit. She began to fan her wings to lower her body temperature, but had no intention of leaving my arm. After a minute or so I decided to gently sit down on the ground. She stayed with me, and the love I was feeling from her ignited tears to stream down my face. I thanked her for this amazing union that we were sharing and expressed love back to her. Our time together lasted for five minutes, upon which she took up flight once again. A truly cherished experience and memory.

A few years back, our neighbor's were having three big pine trees taken down. These pine trees bordered our properties. They provided homes for birds and other wildlife. The trees also gave our neighbor's and us a nice barrier of privacy between our two homes. I was very sad that the trees were being cut down and made sure that I was away from home on the morning of the cut. That afternoon, while sitting on my small back deck feeling down, I looked up to see an owl perched on the wood pole bordering my backyard woods. This beautiful creature just stayed there staring at me. I had wondered if possibly he had a home in one of those downed pine trees. I had heard an owl hooting in the night from that location of our house ever since we built and moved into our downstairs bedroom.

As I continued communing with this Majestic creature, I began to feel empathy for him if he needed to find a new home. If this was the case, then his hardship was certainly greater than mine. It was magical to gaze at one another. This went on for ten minutes or so until, alas, he decided to take flight. It was the flight pattern he took, however, that has me astonished and feeling surreally graced to this day. You see, upon lift off, he began to fly straight towards me. I was mesmerized and frozen in those moments of winged beauty. As he flew closer and closer to me his cheeks were being shaken back and forth with such force that he appeared to have the prune wrinkled face of a very old person. I felt absolutely no fear as he came closer and closer to me. Suddenly, at about a ten-foot length from my face, he swooped up high into the air and over my house. I know that he was comforting me, as possibly I was him. We made a deep connection in the Sacred on that most Holy and wonderous day!

These are just two of my many encounters with our lovely wildlife friends. I am sure that you, as well, have had at least one time of communion experience yourself. We are so blessed for this! As we connect in more Sacred ways with the aliveness in nature we attune to her intelligence, which is that of Spirit as we are.

Mother Teresa often said that she felt closest to God in nature. Saint Francis was so attuned to the natural world that animals flocked to him and rested on his limbs. Stuart Wilde reminds us that we are powerful and positive individuals. We are beautiful. This is a day of balance. We can see only beauty in all people, animals and sentient beings. Each action we take this day is an expression of the God force. There is no real sin, only energy. Lastly, we can affirm for ourselves everyday: I am open at all times to communication from my inner self, which leads me to follow the energy of my highest evolution at all times!

A "New Day" is upon us now. This is a day of great awakening for many, and deeper blossoming, shifting to higher consciousness for others. We must be willing to heal, balance, and restore; if we are to move with the process of living and transformation in our unfolding "New World".

As a child I dreamt a thousand dreams
Of twinkling stars and full moonbeams

The fairies how they danced with grace
And played with me in the secret place

Oh my, the butterflies give airy delight
Till time draws near to take up flight

In this hour that rests upon us now
We grow in wisdom and in meaning

To illuminate with transcendent light
Throughout our very being

This light reaches all who would receive
The healing balm of immortality

Thank you for engaging with me in the teachings of this book. This has been a joyful journey to be "present" as the Divine and my Spiritual Team have Guided me through all of it. I am forever grateful for everything!

Epilogue

I hope you have found inspiration in my journey similar to what I have found while writing this book, sitting by the woods outside of my Vermont home. This is where the picture on the front cover of the book was taken. As your life's journey continues unfolding may you always remember that you are MAGNIFICIENT!! You are genuinely Loved, Cherished and Adored by your Beloved Creator. You are never alone, even when darkness overcomes your mind. Waiting in the Ethers and all about your being is the ever-present Love of ALL, yearning to bring you home. This home is Heaven on Earth, a place where we can BE in Peace and contentment with each passing day. This "SPACE" awaits us all!

Afterword

Another beautifully written and inspiring book by Shari Shea is here for the greater Good of humanity, and I am so grateful. I know first-hand what it is like to be in the Divine Energy that Shari facilitates during a healing service. Shari and her dear father and friends visited us at Unity in the Foothills many times before Covid hit. We were richly and deeply blessed by her healing services, and I eagerly await the time when we can resume "resting in the Spirit" with Shari and all of her Divine assistants. Remarkable, rare, and yet graciously down to earth and available, Shari is one of those Light Workers whose very attunement makes it possible for us to remember that we are also attunable and remarkable. As you read Shari's book, you will no doubt feel within you the Light that is her True Nature and yours. Thank you, Shari! May we all know the blessing of this Very

Light as we continue forward on our sacred pathways.

Namaste.

Rev. Carolyn Swift Jones

Spiritual Leader of Unity in the Foothills

About the Author

Shari devotes her life in Sacred Service to humanity. She has been facilitating Spirit-Led Healing services for many years. Over the past two years her Healing Service work has primarily been with Unity in the Foothills, Torrington, CT. Before the Pandemic, she had begun facilitating services at a Congregational Church in Manchester, CT as well. She has also been known to occasionally lead Healing Services in her home.

Shari is part of Celebrating Life Ministries Interfaith community, whose TRUTH is, "There is only one religion, the religion of LOVE." The work of this Ministry is to help all grow deeper in relationship with Creator, as well as experience Healing and Balance; emotionally, spiritually, and physically.

Shari also works as a Lifestyle Coach and Energy Healer offering private sessions to clients, both in person, as well as by phone and Zoom. She relishes her time with Creator in nature, and finds great pleasure tending to her seasonal vegetable garden.

She lives in Northern Connecticut with her husband. For further information on Shari's healing work visit www.sharishea.com or email sharithree@gmail.com